inclined planes

VALERIE BODDEN

Published by Creative Education
P.O. Box 227, Mankato, Minnesota 56002
Creative Education is an imprint of The Creative Company
www.thecreativecompany.us

Design and production by Liddy Walseth
Art direction by Rita Marshall
Printed by Corporate Graphics in the United States of America

Photographs by Alamy (1, Steven Allan, Ian M Butterfield, Michelle Chaplow,
FB-Studio), Dreamstime (Jan Bruder, Alexander Rochau), Getty Images
(Cristian Baitg, Fritz Goro, Doug Hopfer, Huntstock, Scott Pommier, Robert
Warren), iStockphoto (Steven Allan, Chris Bence, Pattie Calfy, Thomas
Polen, Michal Rozanski)

Library of Congress Cataloging-in-Publication Data
Bodden, Valerie.
Inclined planes / by Valerie Bodden.
p. cm. — (Simple machines)
Summary: A foundational look at inclined planes, explaining how these simple
machines work and describing some common examples, such as ramps, that have
been used throughout history.
Includes index.
ISBN 978-1-60818-008-0
1. Inclined planes—Juvenile literature. I. Title.
TJ147.B6187 2010
621.8'11—dc22   2009048830
CPSIA: 040110 PO1140

First Edition
2 4 6 8 9 7 5 3 1

CREATIVE C EDUCATION

inclined planes

VALERIE BODDEN

contents

Have you ever gone down a slide or sledded down a hill? You might not have known it, but you were using an inclined plane. An inclined plane makes it easier to move objects from one height to another.

An inclined plane is a kind of simple machine. Simple machines have only a few moving parts. Some have no moving parts at all. Simple machines help people do WORK.

Inclined planes get people from place to place

An inclined plane is a flat surface that is higher at one end than the other. A ramp going into a building is an inclined plane. So is a slide at a park.

Inclined planes do not move. Instead, people push objects along them. It is easier to push a heavy object up an inclined plane than to lift it straight off the ground. And objects move easily but not too fast down an inclined plane, too.

The tracks of a roller coaster are made of in-clined planes

The longer an inclined plane is, the flatter its SLOPE. It is easier to move something up a longer, flatter slope. It is harder to move something up a short, STEEP inclined plane. But you do not have to move it as far.

People have been using inclined planes for thousands of years. Almost 5,000 years ago, people in Egypt may have pulled huge stone blocks up ramps to build the **PYRAMIDS** (*PEER-uh-midz*).

Egypt's pyramids are near the city of Cairo (*KY-ro*)

People still use ramps today.
Ramps help people in wheelchairs
get into buildings. They make it
easier to load heavy boxes and
animals onto big trucks, too.

Roads on inclined planes zigzag up mountainsides. They are easier to travel than a road that goes straight up a mountain. Inclined planes make going down water slides and roller coasters fun, too!

The roofs of many buildings are inclined planes. Snow and rain can easily slide off them. Inclined planes are everywhere. Without them, we would have a much harder time moving the objects around us!

Most houses and barns have sloped roofs

A CLOSER LOOK at
Inclined Planes

CLIMB A HILL TO LEARN MORE ABOUT INCLINED PLANES. FIRST, WALK STRAIGHT UP THE HILL. THEN, WALK UP THE HILL IN A ZIGZAG PATTERN. WHICH WAY IS EASIER: WALKING STRAIGHT UP THE HILL OR TAKING A ZIGZAG PATH? ZIGZAG UP THE HILL A FEW MORE TIMES. MAKE YOUR ZIGZAG PATH LONG AND GENTLE ON ONE TRIP. MAKE IT SHORT AND STEEP ON ANOTHER. WHICH PATH DO YOU LIKE THE BEST?

Glossary

pyramids—buildings with three or four triangle-shaped sides
slope—how much something slants, or is tilted, up or down
steep—a slope that goes up or down a lot in a short distance
work—using force (a push or pull) to move an object

Read More

Oxlade, Chris. *Ramps and Wedges.* Chicago: Heinemann Library, 2003.
Thales, Sharon. *Inclined Planes to the Rescue.* Mankato, Minn.: Capstone Press, 2007.

Web Sites

MIKIDS.com
http://www.mikids.com/Smachines.htm
Learn about the six kinds of simple machines and see examples of each one.

Simple Machines
http://staff.harrisonburg.k12.va.us/~mwampole/1-resources/simple-machines/index.html
Try to figure out which common objects are simple machines.

Index